A GRIEF WORKBOOK FOR SKEPTICS

Surviving Loss without Religion

CAROL FIORE

www.flyingkeapress.com

Books by Carol Fiore

Flight through Fire

In memory of experimental test pilot Eric Fiore,
my true love, my best friend, my fellow atheist

$\mathscr{A}$CKNOWLEDGMENTS

$\mathscr{T}$his book began to take shape when I spoke about grief at a Skeptics of Oz conference in Wichita, Kansas. Prior to this, several publishers had told me that nonbelievers sorely needed a grief book—that is, a general guide for atheists. For years I worked on outlines, spoke to others suffering through grief, took notes, wrote hundreds of pages, and scribbled down thoughts in the middle of the night as ideas percolated. I wanted to help others like me, and so this book was born.

I would like to thank my beautiful daughters, Robin and Tia, for their excellent advice and for always believing in me. Thanks also to Kate Eleanor, an incredible friend, writer, and editor. I love you all!

TABLE OF CONTENTS

INTRODUCTION;

OR,

DON'T SKIP THIS PART

You've just lost someone.

Is this book going to say something profound to make your pain go away? No, but give me a chance. Ultimately you'll have to work through the grief yourself, but even a little help is important when you're suffering. I'm not going to tell you there's a God with a plan and a reason for your tragedy. A higher being is not punishing you.

You may call yourself an agnostic, an atheist, a secular humanist, a nonreligious person, or one of the nones.[1] You've been searching for a book that will help you survive your loss. If so, you've picked up the right book. I found no comfort in grief books that explained away pain through a faith in God. In the pages of this book, you'll find tasks to strengthen you, some practical advice,

---

[1] By nones, I mean people who check the box labeled "none" when asked about their religious affiliation on a form or survey.

and the tangible support of a comrade who has suffered too. No God stuff, I promise.

Together we'll tackle our grief. It's difficult, emotionally draining work. I once thought grief was a passive thing, something I had to wait out, but it's not. This book will help you become active in your journey. You'll be flying the plane, not sitting in the back waiting to land.

So what qualifies me to write a book about grief for skeptics? I'm an atheist, and I watched Eric, my husband of twenty years, die thirty-six days after a plane crash in which he lost body parts, including most of his face. He was an experimental test pilot, a dynamic man who rode life with a passion unmatched by most people. After he died, all the help offered to me involved putting my life in the hands of a being I didn't believe in. I had never dealt with grief before, and although I looked diligently, I could find nothing to help me that didn't involve God. I vowed that someday, if I dealt with my grief, I would try to help others like me.

I've written the book I wish I'd had when my husband died. I didn't want any more advice from psychologists, psychiatrists, or counselors. Grief is not well studied and is often misunderstood, so why do mental health and medical professionals—sometimes with no personal grief experience—write most self-help books? I wanted a book written by someone who'd been through it. I wanted a book written by a nonbeliever, an atheist like myself.

I wanted a raw, honest look at grief. I hope this is that book. If you are religious and your faith helps you cope with grief, there are many books out there for you. For the rest of you, I hope this is *your* book.

I designed this book for you to write in. Forget what you were told in school about defacing books; this is a workbook—a guided journal. My most treasured books are the ones in which

I've scribbled in the margins. I encourage you to underline sections and cross out others. Use the blank pages to complete the tasks. As time passes, you may look back at what you've written and realize you're getting better. That's part of what I want to help you achieve.

Now, an important note: I am not a psychiatrist, I am not a counselor, and I have absolutely no experience in the medical field. I do have three science degrees, but my training in meteorology, computer science, and ecology do not qualify me to help you with medical issues. If you or a loved one is suicidal or severely depressed, put this book down *now* and seek medical help. If you're not eating or sleeping and if you're having I-need-to-end-this thoughts, you require help I cannot offer. This book is *not* a substitute for professional help. Instead, think of it as helpful suggestions from a friend.

Okay then.

I'll assume you're reading this book for one of three reasons: (1) you've suffered a loss; (2) a friend or family member has suffered a loss; or (3) you're religious and curious about what an atheist could possibly have to say about grief. If the third reason applies to you, I'm glad you've found this book. We're all members of the same species, and we should—regardless of our religious orientation—help one another. The world could use much, much more tolerance. I try to be mindful of this in my own life and, like most people, must work at it.

This book primarily addresses grief resulting from the death of a loved one, but some of my suggestions could also apply to other types of loss: divorce, unemployment, bankruptcy, foreclosure, or the death of a beloved pet. There are many stressors in our lives, and anything resulting in a profound sense of loss can cause intense sorrow. Grieving nondeath losses doesn't minimize the death of someone you love; they're merely different types of loss.

You can't compare grief; it's all different, because *we're* all different. How can you rate one person's grief against another's? You can't.

One more thing: I want to say those two words you've undoubtedly heard many times by now, but you need to hear them again. *I'm sorry.*

Do I understand what you're going through? A little. After all, I've been there myself, but I'm not you. And you're not me. Nevertheless, together we'll explore death and grief and love and life. Grief is an intensely personal thing, and my experience will not be yours. But perhaps—just perhaps—I can help. Even a little support can make a difference, right? Read on, my friend.

1

GIVING YOURSELF PERMISSION TO GRIEVE

Is your family tired of hearing you talk about your tragedy? Are your friends tired of listening? Are your neighbors and coworkers getting impatient with you? People may be telling you to "hang tough," "stay strong," or "just get through it."

Stop worrying about what other people think. The world may be indifferent to your loss, but you must give yourself permission to grieve. You're not wrong, bad, or defective in any way. You've suffered a profound loss, and it probably feels as though someone has ripped out your insides. You're emotionally devastated. You have a right to be sad. You're grieving not only for the past but also for your lost future.

Don't suppress the pain or try to ignore it. Confront it. Face it. Give yourself permission to feel. Our first task will help you acknowledge your emotions so the healing work can begin.

TASK #1

After you've read this first task, put this book down. Go to a private place where you can be completely alone for a few minutes.

You've been crying a lot. Maybe people have told you to be strong, and you feel guilty for crying. Perhaps you haven't cried at all and people are making you feel bad about that. Forget what people may have said and stop feeling guilty. If you need to cry, do it. Don't force the feelings down. Let them out. That's what this task is about—giving yourself permission to grieve.

Maybe you're not the crying type. You're angry and you want to scream at the world. It's so unfair! Nothing is stopping you. Yell at the top of your lungs if you have to. Shout and curse about the profound sadness you feel. Give yourself permission to do it.

There are so many things you wanted to say to your loved one but never did. Say them now. After my husband Eric died, I talked to him, though I knew he couldn't hear me. Sometimes I yelled at him for leaving, because he had promised he never would. Sometimes I felt guilty for unkind things I had said or done in the past, and I begged his forgiveness. Although this seems at complete odds with atheistic beliefs, it really isn't. Have you ever written a letter, knowing you'd never mail it? Have you ever ranted at the wall, pretending your mean boss was standing there? It was therapeutic, wasn't it?

Come back to this book when you feel ready; cry, scream, or rant. Take your time.

Welcome back. Allow yourself to grieve—crying, screaming, talking, mourning the loss of the future you'd planned. If you don't have a support group, try searching for a local skeptics group.[1] Now, let's take a step toward actively dealing with our grief.

Read this aloud: It may take a long time, but I will get better as time passes. It will not be easy; I will feel like giving up, but I will not. I only have one life; there's no afterlife, this is it. No one ever said it would be easy. Life isn't fair. We all know that.

Giving yourself permission to grieve means you talk about your loss and about your loved one. I feel that this is extremely important. I have met people who put away pictures and reminders of their loved one and refuse to talk about that person. This is not being active in our grieving. Even after thirteen years, I speak at length about my late husband Eric, the experimental test pilot I mentioned in the introduction. Let me tell you something about him now.

Eric hated the expression "Life isn't fair." His retort was, "Fare is something you buy to ride a bus, a plane, or a train." A religious person might tell you there's a reason for your tragedy. Eric would have replied, "Nope. Shit just happens." Thinking about him, telling a short story about him, helps me. I gave myself permission to grieve, and you will too. The next task may help.

---

[1] The Skeptics Groups page at Meetup.com (http://skeptics.meetup.com) is a good place to start.

TASK #2

I've just told you something about Eric. Pretend I'm in the room with you. Tell me something about your loved one. It can be anything. What do you want me to know?

Maybe you miss the way your loved one's eyes crinkled when he or she was happy. Maybe you miss that person's laugh. It doesn't have to be profound. The smallest things are what make a person unforgettable and loved.

Go ahead; I'm listening.

Do you want to cry again? Scream again? It's okay; go ahead.

Grief isn't just about death. It's about rediscovery. Who am I without the person I loved? Grief is a thing, a process—a long one. It isn't a moment in time we face, deal with, and then put behind us. I hate the expression "getting through grief." Grief is not a horrible movie that ends suddenly. It goes on forever. Grief changes the basic structure of our being, and every day we have to deal with it. It's an emotion without end. I usually refer to *grief*, the noun, rather than *grieving*, the verb. When people use the term *grieving*, it sounds like an action you complete—and then, magically, it disappears. It doesn't, which is why I use the noun most of the time—to make it clear it's a *thing*.

Will it get better? Your life will be *different*. Grief is about change, and as time passes, most of us will be better able to cope. The process is different for everyone. Be kind to yourself. Grief is, at its core, about change. And—guess what?—change is hard. But you already know that. Whether it's changing jobs, changing cities, changing schools, or changing friends, it's tough. Now you're experiencing the hardest change of all—life without the person you love. Because we form attachments and put ourselves out there, we get hurt. Loving sometimes means losing, and perhaps that's the most difficult part of life.

Death is universal. Eventually, almost everyone experiences the loss of a loved one. Some of us are more passionate, our emotions are deeper, and our love stronger. That means we're going to experience intense grief more keenly. It also means we're probably stronger. If you're reading this, then you're most likely an atheist or an agnostic. Take comfort in knowing, as you already do, that there isn't a higher power up there punishing you. No one is out to get you. No one is testing you. The gods didn't single you out to blast you with a thunderbolt. There's no plan except the one we humans make. You're not paying penance for some misdeed.

Something terrible has happened to you. That's why it's called a tragedy. The world can be a dark place. Ever wonder why so many books of great literature are tragedies? You're not alone. For a long time, I was convinced that no one had ever suffered as I had. I was wrong. Knowing there are others who are hurting doesn't make your tragedy any easier, but it does mean you're not alone.

You're reading this book because you want to get better. A first step in actively doing something toward that goal is to give yourself permission to grieve: cry, scream, tell stories about your loved one, and surround yourself with a support system of nonreligious friends. Once you've allowed yourself to express your grief and confront the pain you can discover some tools for dealing with it.

2

How Long Will Grief Last?

Grief will last as long as it needs to.

You've probably heard of Elisabeth Kübler-Ross's 1969 signature work *On Death and Dying*, in which she describes the five stages of grief.[1] Although I agree that denial, anger, bargaining, depression, and acceptance can all occur during grief, I do not agree that they all *have* to occur—particularly not in a certain amount of time nor in that order. I don't believe it's healthy to categorize our grief and put labels and time constraints on it; this can actually make us feel that we're grieving "wrongly."

---

[1] Elisabeth Kübler-Ross, *On Death and Dying* (New York: Scribner's, 1997).

If you rush through grief, ahead of your own pace or because others tell you to, you may not be successful in dealing with it. Give yourself time. If you need to keep your loved one's clothes or possessions, keep them. Don't get rid of them because you feel you should. If you get rid of them because you don't need them anymore, it means you've reframed a part of your life without those things—a promising step toward dealing with your grief.

Grief is a very dynamic process. One day you may be unable to get out of bed, the next you may be able to get out and work, the next you are back to feeling sad and overwhelmed. This doesn't mean you aren't making progress; this is part of grief. There are no distinct stages and no set progression to grief.

Grief is a response to a new environment: the world without your loved one. You can't be expected to know how to live in that world right away because grief is a learning process. You're learning how to continue your life and routine without your loved one. If, years after the loss, you are still unable to face the world alone, if every day is still just as hard, you may have what some professionals refer to as *complicated grief*.[2] The important thing is to make progress. Any progress is good, even if it's slow. Look at your grief yourself. Are some days a little easier to get through than they used to be? Can you now look at a photo of your loved one without crying? If there's even one thing you can now do or do better, then you are working on your grief.

Even if you do have complicated grief, it doesn't mean you're going to grieve forever. You may never fully get over your loss, but once you know you aren't making progress, you're in a position to try to do so. It may be more difficult, and you may have to work

---

[2] For information on complicated grief, see the Mayo Clinic, "Complicated Grief: Symptoms," http://www.mayoclinic.com/health/complicated-grief/DS01023/DSECTION=symptoms.

harder at it than people with "normal" grief; for these people progress is often made without trying.

I probably suffer from complicated grief. Progress has been slow, and I have to work at it, but I'm getting better. You can too, my friend.

The activities in this book can help you. If you truly want to heal and learn to live again, you need to work at it. Don't put time constraints on your grief. Grief is pervasive; you may find you can't even go to the post office or eat dinner without feeling like your loved one should be there. Do something you've never done before. It can be small, like cooking something new or watching a movie you've never seen. After you do it, you'll realize you've done something without your loved one. You've just made the first step toward creating a new life without that person. You'll never forget your loved one, but you're strong enough to live in a world without that person in it.

3

$\mathcal{H}$URTFUL STATEMENTS

Do any of these statements sound familiar?

- God doesn't make mistakes.
- You won't get better unless you accept the Lord Jesus Christ into your life.
- God has a plan.
- I'm praying for you.
- Your loved one is in a better place.
- God is testing you.
- There is a reason and a purpose for everything.
- It's God's will.
- Come to my church and pray with me.
- God loves the person you lost.
- God is a kind, just, and caring being.

- Your loved one is happier.
- Have faith.
- Put your life in God's hands.
- It could be worse.
- God never gives us more than we can handle.

There are three main responses to people who say these sorts of things to you: ignore them, fight back, or thank them. What should you do?

I can't answer that question for you because there is no right or wrong answer, but I can tell you what I did. At first, I thanked people because I was in shock, I knew they meant well, and I was trying to be agreeable. As time went by, I became angry about the comments and fought back. I recall snapping at someone, "Why would a loving God force children to watch their father suffer and die?" Eventually I lost the energy to argue with people.

Here are a few possible scenarios. These are some of my actual responses and, admittedly, may not have been the most appropriate. I went through phases, giving different responses based on different people and different circumstances, sometimes going back and forth between anger and acceptance, between tolerance and intolerance. I hid in the atheist closet for most of my life, only coming out when Eric was in the hospital and, even then, not to everyone. Your friends, perhaps even your family, may not know you're a nonbeliever. If you prefer to keep it that way, but don't want to lie or pretend, try the first approach below.

The I-don't-want-to-argue reply

Religious Person (RP): God has a plan.

Me: Thanks. Please excuse me.

The angry reply

RP: Your husband is in a better place.

Me: A hole in the ground is *not* a better place.

The nice-but-assertive reply

RP: Things happen for a reason.

Me: I appreciate your concern, but I don't believe that.

The taking-charge reply

RP: Your husband is with the Lord Jesus.

Me: I respect that you're religious, but I don't believe in an afterlife.

The gentle I'm-an-atheist reply

RP: I'm praying for you.

Me: That's kind, and you've been a great friend. I hope we continue to be friends, but I feel I should be honest. I'm an atheist.

The harsh I'm-an-atheist reply

RP: God never does anything without a reason.

Me: I'm an atheist.

The I'm-not-internalizing-your-comment reply

RP: God never gives us more than we can handle.

Me: Okay.

The advice-to-religious-people reply

RP: Your husband is in heaven and you'll see him again.

Me: I respect your religion, but I'm not a believer. I know you're trying to help me feel better and I appreciate that, but you need only say you're sorry.

The somewhat-rude-and-dismissive reply

RP: Things could be worse.

Me: Sure. Whatever.

This next bit of advice is for people trying to help someone through a loss. It's difficult to know what to say to a friend in emotional pain. Many of us stumble over our words and say the wrong things. We want to help ease the pain, but we know we can't, so we ramble on and on. Sometimes we say inappropriate things. What everyone, religious or nonreligious, needs to say to someone suffering through grief is simple: "I'm sorry." Don't talk about a plan and a better place. Ask what your friend needs. Maybe it's rides for the kids, meals, or errands. The most comforting thing anyone ever said to me was, "My life was better because I knew your husband."

I designed the next task to motivate you to think about appropriate expressions of sympathy that aren't hurtful.

TASK #3

What would you like people to say? What words would give you comfort? Write them below. I believe that someday you will be strong enough to read this to people. You'll be doing them a favor by teaching them what to say to a nonbeliever like yourself. If you are comfortable doing so, share your suggestions with me via e-mail. My website is http://www.carolfiore.com and I'd love to hear your thoughts. I'm also on Twitter @Writer_pilot.

4

You're Stronger Than You Think

The German philosopher Friedrich Nietzsche wrote, "What does not kill me makes me stronger." I disagree when referring to grief. That which doesn't kill us *changes* us, but sometimes not before it shatters us into fragments.

That sounds incredibly depressing, but it's probably how you feel right now, and there's no way to deny the pain. Maybe, in the future, you will feel Nietzsche had it right, or you'll feel you can glue the broken pieces back together. Consider a geode; have you ever broken one open? The crystal interior can be beautiful and surprising; you never know what you'll find. People can be like that too. Occasionally, something amazing results from a breakage. Eric used to say that our character is defined by how well we handle adversity.

Nonbelievers must be strong when facing grief. Wouldn't it be easier to know you'd see your loved one again? Wouldn't it ease the pain, just a bit? This chapter is titled "You're Stronger Than You Think" because you are. Being strong doesn't mean you can't cry, or scream, or rant at the world (recall chapter 1), but it does mean you want to get better, you're going to work at it, and you're going to face it without a fantasy of heaven.

You'll always be different—changed—because of your loss, but you'll be better because you knew and loved that person. Relationships are scary because there is always the potential for loss. Is it worth it?

Yes! Even knowing what I do now, I would still choose to fall in love with Eric.

Perhaps you're shaking your head, wanting to tell me you're not strong. You don't think you can get through life without your loved one. You can. I have done so, and you will too. I designed this next task to prove it.

TASK #4

Find a timer or stopwatch. We're going to count off five minutes. Set the timer.

Sit tall with your spine straight. Clear your mind by concentrating on your breathing. Inhale. Exhale. I know it's going to be hard. Imagine waves rolling onto the warm, white sand of a beach. You hear the soft, lapping sounds of the water.

Take a deep breath.

Count off one minute. Are you thinking of the gentle waves? Picture the swaying palm trees. You hear a gull's cry in the distance.

Another minute has passed. Maybe you were counting seashells. The sun is bright, but there is a calm, cooling breeze.

Three minutes are gone.

A gorgeous tern swoops down to grab a fish.

Four minutes have now passed. The sand is soft under your bare toes. Is that a tiny crab burrowing into a hole near your foot?

Finally, five minutes have passed.

Take another deep breath. You made it. You didn't simply survive five minutes without your loved one, you lived those five minutes in a different way.

As time passes, you'll get better. Some days will be worse than others. You'll slip backward; you'll move forward. Overall, you'll improve. Will *all* the pain go away? Maybe not. Nevertheless, you'll learn to control it, to live with it.

Eventually, a small sliver of light will open. The timing differs for everyone, and the result can be different. Some people will be okay in a short amount of time. Others may take much longer.

This is what your life might look like, and maybe that's as good as it gets. There is a window of light, however small, and you can learn to embrace it.

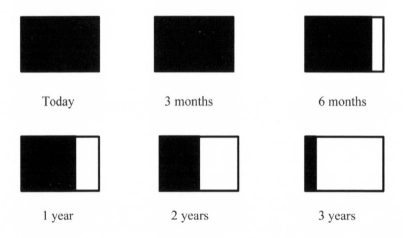

| Today | 3 months | 6 months |

| 1 year | 2 years | 3 years |

I can't tell you how big the box of light will be after ten years, or even twenty. The box may be completely open. Maybe half of it is still dark. Maybe your box is open at less than a year. It's different for everyone. My box, even after thirteen years, contains much darkness. A friend of mine who lost eight loved ones in the course of a year insists that her box was open in less than two years' time.

In the next chapters, you'll learn ways to help strengthen yourself through non-faith-based activities.

5

WHO AM I NOW?

The Greek poet Pindar said, "Become what you are." At forty-one years old, just before Eric's accident, I felt I had at last discovered who I was and what my talents were. I was finally becoming who I was born to be. I thought I was doing it alone, but I was wrong. An amazing person had been helping me for years. Then, in an instant, I lost it all.

I met Eric Fiore when I was eighteen years old. He had just turned twenty. We shared a deep love for aviation; our first date was in an airplane. After three years of dating, we married on a bright spring day. Twenty years and two beautiful daughters later, we had what most would describe as a fairy-tale life. We'd had our hard times, but we'd always remained a team. We used to brag that together we were invincible. I saw Eric through two college degrees; after graduation, he worked hard to become an F-15 fighter pilot, then on to become a well-respected experimental test pilot for Bombardier Flight Test. He helped me run a marathon, earn two graduate degrees, and acquire my own flight ratings. He was always there, and he encouraged me, telling me I could achieve anything. He was supportive through medical crises, two pregnancies, and the many trials of life. He never quit helping me, loving me, believing in me. I'd always loved him, but I never understood the depth to which I identified with him and the extent to which many of his personality traits became my own. When he died, my identity and the confidence he had helped to build and nurture withered and dried up. Like a dead tree branch in a raging storm, I crashed to the ground.

After Eric died, there was the expected depression and withdrawal. When I began to venture out of the house again, there was an almost manic obsession with keeping Eric's memory alive. He'd once said, "There is nothing worse than dying and being forgotten." These words controlled my life. My normally obsessive personality drove this need to the exclusion of everything except the care of my two daughters. My needs, my wants, my likes, didn't matter anymore.

Eric liked golf, and even though I never had, I took lessons. I used his clubs, refusing the teacher's advice to buy ones that fit me. I started flying again after many years of waning interest. I started to quote Eric's political views as though they were my own. I voted for his party in the election, not mine. I enforced rules on our daughters that I thought Eric would approve of. Although I had once been an avid bird watcher, I lost interest in my avian friends. I stopped running. I didn't read ecology books anymore. I couldn't wait to go to sleep, where—at least in my dreams—Eric lived again.

I struggled to find a way to get my old life back. How could I reassemble the pieces of what had been a well-charted and orderly life? It took years to realize that the key was not in finding myself but in re-creating myself. You can't go back.

I had to rebuild a self-identity that did not include Eric. I rejected the advice that I needed a new man to make me happy. First, I had to learn to give myself permission to say, honestly, what I liked or wanted and not what Eric would have liked or wanted. I tried meditating, but that didn't work for me. I found some comfort in reading basic philosophy texts. I took long walks with my dogs and looked at the changing fall colors, the rabbits hopping through the brush, the elk grazing calmly in my yard. I did volunteer work. I exercised. I spent a large portion of each day writing about Eric and trying to remember the good times.

There was much self-reflection.

The screen saver on my computer consists of pictures of Eric, some of the two of us together. If my attention wanders, or if I'm not working diligently on some task, my screen saver kicks in and suddenly images of Eric pass before me. My grief is similar—always waiting in the background, ready to come back at any moment. Sometimes I see images of myself and I don't realize it's me. Where is that person, I wonder? Perhaps grieving means saying good-bye twice—once to my husband and once to the old me.

Now I'm on a journey of rediscovery—becoming who I am *now*. This time the trek is different; I'm not the same person I was before the accident. Living with Eric for so many years changed me in profound ways, and losing him took away more than a husband.

I'm done with my story now, and it's time for yours.

TASK #5

What were some of your loved one's favorite activities? Make a list. Then make a list of your own favorite activities.

Which activities are on both lists? Circle them. Do you feel that engaging in those activities would make you sad? If you said yes, then pick one that's only on your list, and think about doing it. Maybe it's repairing cars, or painting. Do you feel like doing that now? If you said no, it's okay. You'll feel like doing it again one day, but maybe today is not that day. And maybe tomorrow isn't either—and that's okay too. Recall chapter 2: there are no time constraints.

When you're suffering, losing interest in old activities is normal. You don't have the energy or motivation to do anything. Depression is part of the grief process, but if it goes on too long, consider getting help. It's difficult to say precisely how long "too long" is; again, everybody's different. If you've stagnated and aren't making improvements—even small ones—that's an indication of a problem; it could be a sign of complicated grief, which I briefly mentioned in chapter 2.[1]

How do you feel about doing something new that isn't on either list? Perhaps you've always wanted to visit the local art museum but never found the time.

Maybe today is a good time to start working on a new identity.

---

[1] Take a look at the Center for Complicated Grief's website, http://www.complicatedgrief.org, or "Complicated Grief," *Harvard Medical School Family Health Guide*, http://www.health.harvard.edu/fhg/updates/Complicated-grief.shtml.

$\mathcal{F}$AVORITE $\mathcal{A}$CTIVITIES

My Loved One's Favorites	My Favorites

When you live with someone, you lose some of your independence, but sacrificing a small piece of yourself can result in something stronger. Love is a fusion of two people, which is both scary and wonderful. The people we live with shape us.

It will take time to re-create yourself. Be patient. If you want to try an activity from your loved one's list that you never really liked, that's okay too. I'm not sorry I tried golf. Someday you'll return to your previous activities, though perhaps not all of them. You'll find new things on your odyssey of self-discovery. I never knew before Eric's death how much I would love to write.

For now, take small steps. You're learning to live without your loved one. You may think you can't do it, that you can never accomplish anything without that person, but you're wrong. Recall Pindar's words and think of the new and interesting things you will discover about yourself.

6

HEALTH ISSUES

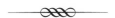

I'm not a doctor. Please bear that in mind when you read this chapter. It's not a bad idea to get a checkup, perhaps blood work and any other tests you've been putting off. Grief imposes serious stress on the body and can cause a variety of problems—some physical, some mental. My family pestered me about having a complete medical workup, so I did. Make your family happy and do it.

Weight loss or gain after a tragedy is common, but if it turns into a problem, you need to seek help. I eventually started eating again after a weight loss of about fifteen pounds (I weighed 118 at the time of Eric's accident), but my older daughter, Tia, developed a binge-eating disorder that required years of treatment; it's still a problem today.

Insomnia is common after a shock. Be careful with habit-forming sleep medications. It's much better to develop a bedtime routine (drinking a cup of decaffeinated tea, reading a calming book, using a sound generator, maintaining a quiet and dark bedroom). Try to avoid watching violent or disturbing movies or having long phone conversations about your loved one before bed. Meditation and yoga take practice, but the effort can be worth it.

Now we come to the question you really want to ask. Should I take an antidepressant? If you were on one before the tragedy, now is not the time to stop. However, if you have never been on an antidepressant and your family and friends urge you to take one now, please think carefully and consult more than one doctor before deciding. A pill cannot fix everything.

Some people are genuinely ill and need medication. However, I don't believe that otherwise healthy people making their way through difficult times need to be on drugs. Antidepressants aren't the answer to everything; they're not going to give you a better life. In my opinion, it's wrong to give these drugs to healthy, stable people experiencing grief.

About ten months after my husband's death, a few family members and various counselors convinced me to climb aboard the happy pill train. Why? They thought I was too sad, though I had made no suicide attempts and had no history of mental illness of any kind. They hadn't witnessed this type of profound sadness in anyone, and they didn't know how to handle it. One of my sisters remarked to a friend, "I don't know what to do to help her. She just wants to talk about Eric all the time."

The grief process began to slow down after a few weeks on Prozac. I found I didn't cry as much, but I was tired all the time. I'm normally an energetic person, and I had no drive. I went about my daily chores in a daze, devoid of any passion. I'm usually an opinionated and forceful person, with strong convictions, but

I was now allowing people to lead me around and tell me what to do. I made poor choices, was taken advantage of, and failed to stand up for myself. Tia discovered she could do anything she wanted and get away with it. My younger daughter, Robin, didn't understand why I was in bed by eight o'clock every night.

For over two years I took the medication. One day, through my Prozac haze, I had an epiphany. I looked in the mirror and didn't recognize the face staring back at me, didn't see the woman my husband had been so proud of. Instead, I saw a spineless zombie addicted to pills. I took all the Prozac in the house and returned it to the clinic.[1]

Many doctors say you shouldn't suddenly go off Prozac. After a couple weeks, I felt suicidal. The grief and the extreme sadness came tumbling back. It was as if I'd never worked through it at all. I should never have been on the pills, but I most certainly should not have stopped so abruptly.

Grief is not a disease requiring pills. Think carefully before you rush to board the happy pill train. You're hurting, you're in pain, and you want it to go away. That's understandable, believe me, but antidepressants may not be the answer. Using other drugs, excessive alcohol consumption, cutting, and dozens of other self-destructive behaviors are not the answer either. If you're even considering engaging in these types of activities to numb your emotions, you must seek help. *Do it now.*

Grief is painful, but there's no choice. No pill, no bottle, is going to make it go away.

---

[1] The US Food and Drug Administration publishes guidelines for safe disposal of medicines at http://www.fda.gov/drugs/resourcesforyou/consumers/ buyingusingmedicinesafely/ensuringsafeuseofmedicine/safedisposalofmedicines/ ucm186187.htm.

TASK #6

It's bedtime, and you can't sleep. Again.

What activity used to make you laugh or smile? Maybe you pop in an old comedy movie and curl up on the sofa with a soft blanket. Maybe you reach for a book with pictures of silly animals. Maybe you sit in a darkened room, on the floor, with your legs crossed and your mind blank. Maybe you play, softly, a CD of soothing sounds.

Think about a healthy activity that helps you relax—one that doesn't reflect on your loved one. Avoid caffeine. Maybe bedtime isn't the best time to eat that carton of chocolate-coffee ice cream. What about a cup of chamomile tea? Don't be hard on yourself if it doesn't work. You'll try again tomorrow night.

Now, a harsh statement: Life without passion is not worth living, but you *must* give yourself time to heal. The passion will return, but it may take time. Be patient; be kind to yourself. If you have to pump drugs (not prescribed by a doctor) into your body to deaden your senses, you might as well be dead. And I know you don't want to be dead. Like me, you're a nonbeliever and you know you only have one life. Only one. This is it. Are you going to give it up so easily? Or will you fight for it? It won't be easy, but you can do it.

Fight.

Do it without putting bad shit in your body.

7

ℋELPING ℋIDS

Losing a parent or sibling as a child is a life-transforming event. My daughters Robin and Tia, who were ten and thirteen at the time of the accident, would agree: watching their father die changed their lives. Children need special attention and perhaps counseling. It can be difficult to provide this if you're suffering too. If you're unable to care for them, get help: family, friends, school counselors, teachers, and neighbors can all assist you. Children may be grieving but unable to express it. Let them talk and, when possible, answer their questions with your own— questions directed at helping them: "What do you think? How do you feel? What can I do to help you?"

If you're a parent who has lost a child, allow me to say how very sorry I am for your loss. Losing a child is probably the worst pain a person can experience. As my mother-in-law said after the death of my husband, her oldest son, "No parent should have to bury a child." Simply saying "I'm sorry" seems insufficient in the face of such agony. There are support groups out there; please consider attending a meeting if you've lost a child. Contact your local hospital or physician, a hospice group,[1] or organizations associated with the cause of death (such as the American Cancer Society[2]) for phone numbers of local support groups. State departments of health or social services may also be of help. There are groups for grieving parents who have lost a child to disease, suicide, murder, and drunk drivers. The Centering Corporation provides grief help and publishes a magazine called *Grief Digest*.[3] Robin and I have both published articles in this magazine; be aware, however, that some stories are religion-based.

Compassionate Friends is another organization that provides help for parents and siblings who've lost a young family member.[4] Their website says they have no religious affiliation, but of course, some members will be religious, and meetings are often held in local churches.

This chapter is not about losing a child. It's about taking care of children after a tragedy, so if you're not a caregiver, feel free to skip to chapter 8.

It can be difficult for nonbelievers to help a child who desperately wants to believe in heaven. Perhaps others have already convinced the child of God's plan. You don't want to lie or pretend to believe something you don't, but you also don't want to take away a child's fantasy of seeing a loved one again. Many atheists

---

[1] For information on local hospice chapters and bereavement counselors, go to HospiceNet, http://www.hospicenet.org.

[2] See, for example, "Resources for Parents and Families Who Have Lost a Child to Cancer," http://www.cancer.org/treatment/childrenandcancer/whenyourchildhascancer/resources-for-parents-and-families-who-have-lost-a-child-to-cancer.

[3] The Centering Corporation, http://www.centering.org.

[4] Compassionate Friends, http://www.compassionatefriends.org.

probably believed in religion and God as a child. I did, but not my husband Eric. My suggestion is to let a child believe whatever will help. You should be listening instead of talking anyway.

Your kids may wake up with nightmares or be unable to sleep; they may develop anger problems. They may lose interest in activities and friends, their grades may drop, and appetite changes may occur. Constant crying, withdrawal, and refusal to get out of bed can be signs of a serious problem. I suggest that a counselor be consulted but—just as for yourself—be careful about allowing drugs to be given to your kids.

TASK #7

Search the Internet,[5] a bookstore, or the library; consult teachers and school counselors for an age-appropriate book dealing with loss. Support groups may be able to provide a list of books. If your children believe in God, there are plenty of books; if not, you'll have a more difficult time finding material. I suggest you first read any book you intend to give to your child. Again, you'll have to consider the age of the child; this is where a teacher can be helpful.

Have you located a book? Read it together, discuss it, and assure your child that there isn't anything wrong with grieving. If you are both up to it, do activities together like baking cookies, going for a hike, or making crafts. This may be the perfect time to discuss the death.

---

[5] Entering the search phrase "grief books for children" at http://www.amazon.com brings up a long list of books. You will have to determine which are appropriate for your child; many or all may contain religious ideas.

Kiss your child. Say those three all-important words, "I love you." Reassure your child that you will be here tomorrow, because right now, that is probably her biggest fear. If the child has lost a sibling, she may be fearful of dying too.

When should children go back to school? When should they resume their normal activities? I let Tia and Robin tell me when they were ready. Their teachers let homework assignments slide and granted special concessions they didn't give other kids. Robin rejected the special treatment, whereas Tia took advantage of it. Just don't let it go on too long; you may be setting a child up for a lifetime of being a victim. If you need help regarding when to resume a more normal schedule, talk to teachers or a counselor.

Be observant. Certain behavior changes are normal, but things like binge eating and drug or alcohol abuse are cries for help. Get them help. I listened closely to the music my girls played. This can tell you much about children's feelings and emotional state. Has your child dumped old friends? Acquired new friends? Become a loner?

Try to be there for them, though I know that's difficult. You're grieving too. I wasn't always there emotionally for my girls. I sometimes blame it on the Prozac, but it was a combination of things. I had choices, and often I didn't make the right one. For instance, when Tia demanded I allow her to attend parties I knew were inappropriate, I let her. I was too tired and sad to fight her about everything, so I gave in. I paid the price, as did she, and I now regret not being stricter.

Robin had just turned ten when she had to watch her father die; about children, she now says, "Let them grieve. Don't take it away."[6]

---

[6] Robin R. Fiore, "Thank You, Flint," *Grief Digest* 10, no. 3 (2012): 24-25.

8

SUPPORT GROUPS AND COUNSELORS

$\mathcal{M}$ost of us need help when we're grieving. Isn't that why you're reading this book? Unfortunately, after a death, entire family dynamics can change for the worse. Parents, in-laws, siblings, and other relatives can become embroiled in ugly fights for money and possessions. Many of us have seen it happen. Perhaps the entire family needs counseling, either individually or in a group setting. Grief can often destroy families, but I've seen it pull them together too. I sincerely hope yours is the latter case.

I saw five different counselors and two psychiatrists. I lost track of the vast number of doctors and counselors Tia visited; she also participated in group sessions. She became a master at manipulating mental health people, whereas Robin simply refused to talk to the one counselor forced on her.

In retrospect, I should have attended support groups, as they would have been far more beneficial than the multitude of counselors who continued to ask, "How do you feel?" The psychiatrists threw drugs at me and then presented me with bills.

Individual mental health professionals didn't really help the three of us, though I'm sure they can be extremely important for some; the key is in finding the right one. My suggestion is to try it; get a recommendation, if possible. If the first doesn't work out, try a different one.

There are support groups for a wide range of issues. Check your local newspaper or try the Internet. Give your local hospital a call or ask your family doctor. If a group meeting face-to-face doesn't appeal to you, how about an online help group? Sometimes Facebook and Twitter friends can help, but be careful about giving out personal information. There are unscrupulous people out there who will take advantage of your grief. Guard your privacy with great care.

About a year and a half after Eric died, I joined a writing group, and then years later, I went back to school, taking creative nonfiction classes. That helped more than any counselor did; writing can be extremely therapeutic. You may already have a wonderful support group in the way of family, friends, and colleagues. Don't be afraid to ask people for help.

What is it that you need? Maybe it's as simple as getting out of the house and going to lunch. *Ask.* I believe you'll find that people want to help; they just don't know what to do. So tell them what you need.

TASK #8

Do you need help? Be honest; you probably do. Do you have the resources to pay for mental health counseling? If not, or if this is not the right choice for you, get on the phone, call your family doctor or local hospital, and ask about a support group. Call hospice organizations for advice. When is the next meeting? Write it on your calendar. Try to attend.

Get on the Internet. Start searching for support groups. Be aware that many grief groups revolve around a trust and faith in God. You may have to search diligently to find something that will work for you. Look at the excellent Facebook page Grief Beyond Belief.[1]

If none of that works, do what I did: call your local community center or college and inquire about creative nonfiction writing groups. You can always audit the class if the thought of grades and tests scare you. You may well find yourself in the company of others who are suffering; in one of the writing groups I participated in, I met a woman who had lost not only her husband but also her daughter. My good friend Kate, who I met in a writing workshop, lost her sister in a car accident when they were both young teenagers. If you encounter others who are grieving, you'll discover you're not alone.

One day, grief calls for us all.

---

[1] Grief Beyond Belief, https://www.facebook.com/faithfreegriefsupport.

NOTES: INTERNET RESOURCES, PHONE CALLS, SUPPORT GROUPS

9

HOLIDAYS AND ANNIVERSARIES

I never realized how many personally important anniversaries there were until I tried to avoid them: the anniversary of Eric's accident and of his death, his birthday, the day we met, our first date, our wedding anniversary . . . The list was unending. Then there were the holidays like Valentine's Day (also my birthday), Father's Day, and Halloween (Eric's favorite).

I ran away from Christmas for years—literally. The kids and I left town. I refused to go to a restaurant on my Valentine's Day birthday; I didn't want to see other women, laughing and in love, who hadn't lost their spouse or partner. I wept on Father's Day because my children had no daddy to dress up in a silly tie. I refused to carve pumpkins on Halloween because Eric had always done it. I ignored Thanksgiving.

As the years passed, things slowly improved. I finally stayed home for Christmas, even baking Eric's favorite cookies. I dressed up on Halloween. I allowed my daughters to take me to a restaurant on my birthday. It was still difficult, but the pain became a dull ache rather than a roar of anguish. The despair I feel on the anniversary of Eric's death has never eased; I fret that, aside from the family, people don't remember Eric. But then I think about Margaret and Stephan.

Every year close to the anniversary of Eric's accident, a former coworker of his named Margaret sends me a card. She writes about Eric's amazing life and asks how the girls and I are doing. I cherish her card and it hangs on my refrigerator for weeks. I rejoice because someone has remembered.

Perhaps others think of the girls and me on this day but are afraid to send a note. Maybe they think I have forgotten the date and that their expression of sympathy will bring back sad memories. I'd like to assure them that I haven't forgotten. I will never forget what day it was that Eric died. I'm sure some grieving people would prefer not to receive a note like this every year; my in-laws probably would not. If you're thinking about contacting someone who's lost a loved one, I suggest you contact that person at a time that is removed from the anniversary. You could say something like, "I think about you every year at this time, but I'm unsure if you'd like me to contact you. Please tell me what would make you most comfortable." There. You asked. You may or may not be surprised at the response, but either way you'll know how to proceed.

My husband Eric had a protégé and pilot friend named Stephan. Once over coffee, Eric told Stephan a story about how he and I struggled to pay bills when we were young students. Eric would take me to the local mall on Friday night and buy me a single piece of See's chocolate because it was all we could afford. The first Christmas after Eric died, I received a box of See's chocolates from Stephan and his family with a note explaining that Eric had told him the story. Every single year, Stephan sends us See's chocolates. It has become such a tradition that Tia recently remarked, "You can't depend on much in life except that Stephan's candy will come." Saying thanks to Stephan, and to Margaret, doesn't seem like enough for the kindness they have shown all these years.

If you're the friend or family member of a grieving skeptic, then please, *please* don't offer prayers on that special day or, like my Catholic mother, say you're having a mass said in honor of the loved one who died. For the past thirteen years, my mother has sent me several prayer cards listing the date the parish priest was saying a mass in Eric's honor. She knows Eric was an atheist; she knows I'm an atheist. This may bring my mother some comfort, but for me it is more than hurtful—it's disrespectful and mean. Try these words if you're the friend of a grieving skeptic: "I'm thinking of you on this difficult day." That's enough.

Holidays and anniversaries are particularly tough when you've lost a loved one. Remember chapter 5, on re-creating yourself? Perhaps it's time to come up with a new tradition on these difficult days. You don't have to get rid of the old customs; just add a new one or two, even putting the former ones on hold for a while. In time, these holidays will get easier.

10

READING, WRITING, AND THE ARTS

The humanities are, perhaps, one of our greatest achievements. Literature, art, philosophy, and language make our lives rich, unique, and beautiful. Art embodies our internal struggles and our deepest emotions. In interpreting various art forms, we're often forced into introspection, and that's a good thing when suffering through grief. When experiencing art, we can be passive in what we do, whether that be reading, watching musical theater, or observing someone paint or sculpt. Those of us who are talented in the arts can be more active, such as singing, painting, or writing ourselves. Whichever you choose, let the magic of the arts wash through you and help you heal. Let's start with the most basic—reading.

You may want to shout at me, "I can't concentrate on the smallest detail, let alone read a book! I'm lucky if I can get through a few newspaper sentences." The same thing happened to me. I have three university degrees, and for months after Eric died, I couldn't get through a paragraph of the simplest text. Your thoughts are scattered and jumbled; your mind wanders. *What did I just read?* It happens to many of us. The next task may help with the frustration you might be feeling.

TASK #9

Have you been trying to read one of those difficult masterpieces? Or maybe a technical manual? Are you frustrated and angry with yourself? Put the book away. Just for a while.

Take a deep breath. You'll be able to finish your book one day, and you can go back to reading the classics, or whatever genre interests you most. Today might not be that day.

Maybe you love to read. Reading is your solace, your way of escaping. You're an artful reader, savoring every word. However, if you can't concentrate on the words, it's going to become a source of stress and frustration. If your mind can't stay focused, do something else.

Try something simple: go for a walk, listen to music, watch a silly movie, give your dog a hug.

I know that was difficult, but give yourself time and you'll be reading your favorites again. You're reading this book, aren't you? That's a start.

People sometimes ask me for book recommendations. I hesitate because my tastes could be quite different from yours. I had trouble reading and concentrating for a long time, but when I could handle reading again, I found the most comfort in basic philosophy texts and books by existentialists like Albert Camus. I'm a huge fan of his book *The Plague*.

You may find yourself drawn to memoirs. I avoided memoirs after Eric died, perhaps because the ones I found were overly religious or because they attempted to be deep in a phony, trite, or forced manner. What I wanted was the truth—not some lame attempt at a profound philosophy. I wanted raw, open honesty. But years later, after Eric's death, I actively sought memoirs out.[1]

Spend some time in the bookstore, or at the library, or at online bookseller sites. I tend to lean toward the Russians for inspiration. They know and understand suffering in a way I relate to; also, I've spent time in the country—both the former USSR and modern-day Russia. Although many of the Russian classic writers were religious, there is still inspiration and truth for you to discover. I don't believe this is at odds with atheistic views. I find parts of the Bible well written, even poetic; I simply read it as a work of fiction. One of my favorite books and theater productions is Victor Hugo's *Les Misérables*, clearly a religious work of literature. I'm also inspired by the words of Antoine de Saint-Exupéry, a religious man, in his masterpiece *The Little Prince*.

My favorite short story dealing with death is Leo Tolstoy's "Death of Ivan Ilyich." It's not for everyone, and definitely not something you'll want to read immediately after a tragedy, but keep it in mind when you're looking for something new. It's an intense look at death, and in my opinion is a masterpiece. It's easy to read and you will keep reading.

---

[1] My favorite memoir is Lucy Grealy's *Autobiography of a Face* (New York: Harper Perennial, 2003). It's poignant without being overly sentimental or self-pitying.

What about writing, a more active pursuit?

If you haven't written thank-you notes to people who've helped you out, maybe now is the time to start. Have a friend buy you some cards and stamps and get writing. Your notes don't have to be long. I know sending cards is out of fashion, but it's much more personal than sending an e-mail or a text message. Try it.

I know you don't want to do this type of writing. You might even want to shout, "You know what I want to write? I want to write about my loved one!"

What's stopping you? Remember, you never have to show your words to anyone. You have many options. I started by writing happy memories of Eric in short pieces. I began doing this right after he died. I wrote over sixty stories, and joined a writing group less than two years after his death. As the years passed, I began incorporating the stories into a broader work. I wrote every day; sometimes I wrote all night. Writing became my life: I attended writing workshops; I went back to college to take formal writing classes; I hung out at bookstores; I studied the writing market; I spent my evenings reading grammar books; I wrote a book proposal; I sent out query letters to agents and publishers for the book I'd written about Eric.

If I was lucky I received rejection letters. Most of the time publishers and agents ignored my submissions. Finally, a magazine published one of my stories. I continued sending query letters. I got more rejection letters, or none at all. I hoped. I despaired. I spent years of my life trying to become a writer. I was able to get a few more magazine articles published.

A literary agent finally signed me on. He got rejection letters. More years went by, and I lost hope. I continued to read grammar books, and I spent four to six hours a day writing—sometimes more.

I began to write a young adult fiction trilogy, hoping it would be more marketable than my book about Eric's death. For the first time, I couldn't wait to write; my fictional characters jumped out of the pages and directed me. They became my friends, and I wanted them to live in the pages of a published book. I started the query process anew, but this time it was for my fiction book, not the one about Eric.

I finally terminated the contract with my literary agent, who had given up anyway, and I started the process all over to find a new agent to promote the book about Eric. The rejection letters rolled in.

In April 2012, I got a simultaneous request from two different publishers to read each of my books: the first book of the young adult fiction trilogy and the book about Eric. Unfortunately, it didn't work out with either of them. I started over again.

At the beginning of 2014, I finally published *Flight through Fire*,[2] the book about Eric. I'd spent over a decade working on it.

Do you really want to do this?

Trying to publish a book has been the most frustrating and disappointing experience of my life. The constant barrage of rejections began to wear me down and to erode my self-confidence. However, my financial situation allowed me to spend years doing it, and I had the full support of my children. I'm extremely disciplined. I didn't look for excuses to get out of writing.

Consider writing for yourself or your family, but if you feel you must publish, as I did, self-publishing is an option and seems to have lost the stigma it once had. Be aware, you'll have to do your

---

[2] *Flight through Fire* is available in paperback and on Kindle at http://www.amazon.com and in paperback at http://www.barnesandnoble.com and at other sites.

own marketing; the average number of books sold by the self-publisher is quite low.

TASK #10

Without planning or thinking too deeply, write one page about your loved one. It doesn't have to be a story with a plot. It can consist of rambling thoughts.

If you prefer, write a letter. Maybe you're angry with your loved one for leaving you. That's okay. Write it down. Put it away until tomorrow.

THOUGHTS ABOUT MY LOVED ONE

Is it the next day? Read what you wrote. Do you feel like writing more? If so, buy a journal. It doesn't have to be expensive; a spiral notebook will do. Set aside a certain time every day for writing. If you prefer to use your computer, that's also an option. Perhaps you'll publish someday, but make sure you do it for the right reason. Money is not the right reason; you won't get rich at it. But I published, so why not you too?

Writing can be excellent therapy, but so can art and music. Consider expressing yourself through those outlets. Sculpting, painting, and community musical theater are just a few options. Have you considered learning a foreign language, joining a book club, or taking a pottery class? Visit an art museum or take an opera appreciation course. Learn to play an instrument. Step away from your grief and immerse yourself in something engaging, artistic, compelling. Discover something new about yourself and the world.

1 1

ℰXERCISE

ℐ 've been a competitive long-distance runner since my early twenties. Running has been such an important part of my life that I defined myself by it: "I'm a runner" was often the first sentence out of my mouth when meeting someone.

After Eric died, I lost interest in running. Eventually I got back out on the road, but it was never the same again. I didn't care about winning races anymore, but it was more than that. The thing I loved about running—being alone with my thoughts—became the thing I hated most. I didn't want to be alone with my thoughts; I wanted to forget them. The self-reflection I'd always cherished about running began to kill me. Then I did something that truly focused competitive runners never do. I ran with portable music. My goal was to drown out the voices and the thoughts. At home, I played music too loudly or played movies I'd seen many times before. Background noise of any kind muffled the screams inside my heart.

As time passed I was able to go back to running, alone with my thoughts, but the sport had changed for me. My body had grown older; past injuries and new ones crept up on me. I tried Pilates, which I loved, and yoga, which I had to force myself to do—the meditation part was difficult. I acquired a mountain bike, joined a local health club, and started lifting weights. I took group exercise classes and met new people. I became fond of the elliptical machine because it didn't hurt my damaged knees and torn ligaments.

Doctors tout exercise as beneficial for your heart, your health, and your mind. I have always been an exercise fanatic, and it has been good for me. I didn't realize how much I used running to handle stress in my life until I stopped doing it.

I believe you too can find an activity that will help you. Consult a doctor before starting on any exercise routine, particularly if you have physical disabilities or other issues. Running, in my case, has proved to be hard on my joints—especially my knees. My best friend is a swimmer and she raves about the benefits of it, telling me it would be easier on my knees. I've never been fond of being in the water, so I haven't taken her up on her invitation to the pool. She keeps trying, and perhaps one of these days I'll try it. This next task should get you thinking about your own fitness.

TASK #11

*Are you a member of your local health club or community center?
If not, do you have the funds to join? Consider paying it a visit;
check out the classes and equipment.*

*Is there an activity that is of interest in the list below? These
are just a few of the many options available. Try one. There are
groups that participate in almost all the things I've listed, so if
you'd prefer not to go solo, call your local community center or
search the Internet for a local club or group.*

- Walk, jog, or run (on a treadmill, on the road, in a park, in a mall).
- Hike (consider taking a friend or a dog).
- Get an exercise workout video and do it in your home.
- Cycle.
- Swim.
- Join a tennis or racquetball league.
- Try Pilates or yoga (in a group class; or rent, buy, or borrow a video).
- Take up skiing (cross-country doesn't require expensive lift tickets).
- Try weight lifting (start light).
- Take martial arts or group combat classes.
- Try volleyball, softball, soccer, baseball, or other group sports.
- Try roller-skating, roller-blading, or table tennis; these are good family activities that can be done with the kids.

NOTES: SPORTS, PHYSICAL ACTIVITIES, CLASSES

Did you blow off this task? Did you tell yourself you'd exercise tomorrow? Did you convince yourself you're too old or too fat to do any of the activities I listed?

Did you answer yes to any or all the questions above?

Hmmmm. Then you're going to do the next task.

TASK #12

If there are kids under your care, get a babysitter to watch them for half an hour. Grab a comfortable pair of shoes. Collect a coat and hat if you need them and an umbrella too. Rain is not going to be an excuse; I lived in the Netherlands for three years and the Dutch never use rain as an excuse for anything.

Go for a short walk.

Admit it. You feel better, don't you? Promise yourself you'll do it again tomorrow. If you need to silence the voices, bring some portable music or a friend. I believe in exercise as a major tool you can use for lessening your grief, plus studies show it is good for you.[1]

---

[1] See, for example, http://www.hsph.harvard.edu/nutritionsource/staying-active-full-story/

12

THE POWER OF NATURE

Emily Dickinson's famous Poem 254 starts out "Hope is the thing with feathers." It holds special meaning for me because I am a birder, a bird pet owner, a former bird zookeeper, and a lover of all things avian. My feathered friends have done much over the years to help me in my grieving and to restore some measure of hope for my future. Whether it's watching wild birds, laughing at the antics of my pet duck, or snuggling with my lovable Moluccan cockatoo, I've discovered a comfort and richness in being near them. I feel at once privileged and in awe. Perhaps I'm drawn to birds, more than other groups of animals, because of my love of aviation. Eric was a pilot. I'm a licensed pilot. Our first date was in an airplane.

I find happiness in the world of birds; they bring me hope. Nature is one of the most powerful and important tools I use in handling my own grief.

There is great comfort in watching wild animals. Remember how you felt the first time you saw a deer? That sense of joy and wonder stays with you. As you think back on it, embrace it; wrap it around yourself. As children, we delight in discovering a croaking toad, a salamander sloshing through the mud, a baby squirrel scampering up a tree. We run through fields and pick wildflowers, weaving them into crowns. We fill our pockets with rocks and seashells. What a shame that we often forget nature's wondrous gifts.

Concentrate on rediscovering that joy. It will help you heal.

I can almost hear you now, about to move on to the next chapter in disgust. "I live in New York City!" you may be shouting. "There are only pigeons here!" Alternatively, you may be shrugging, thinking *I'm not an animal person.*

Do you have a computer? Access to the Internet? If so, you can find animal photos, movies, and documentaries. This next assignment is for you if you are the housebound, city-dwelling, indifferent-to-nature type.

TASK #13

Have a friend bring you an animal picture book, preferably one with animals that "sort of" interest you. Maybe you've always wanted to go to the Serengeti. Maybe coral reefs fascinate you. We all love penguins, right?

If you have access to the Internet, search for funny animal pictures or read about an animal that looks interesting. I highly suggest a website called the Daily Squee at http://icanhas.cheezburger.com/squee.

Check out Amazon, Netflix, or other sites for available movies or documentaries on animals. PBS's Nature series is an option, and of course, there are many reality animal shows to choose, if you like that type of programming.

Still not interested in animals? Look at pictures of beautiful landscapes instead. What landscape do you prefer—the beach, mountains, rolling farmlands, rugged highlands, desert? We live on a diverse planet, and there are coffee table books available for almost every country; you're bound to find a few you like.

Shut your eyes and imagine, for just a moment, that you are in one of these places. Can you feel the sun, the breeze? What do you smell? Is that a coyote howling?

If you live outside the city, it's time to talk about going outside. Your task is simple: get out there!

TASK #14

Go for a walk or hike. Don't take any portable music this time.

What type of environment do you live in? Are you familiar with the term ecosystem? Take a good look around you. Although it might not seem so at first glance, even the desert is teeming with life. Do you see any animals? Can you identify any of them? What about the vegetation?

Look up at the sky. Can you identify the types of clouds? Is that a flock of birds? Shut your eyes for a moment. Are those flowers you smell? What sounds are floating your way?

Try to look at the setting as if you were going to paint it, write about it, or describe it in perfect detail to a friend.

Absorb it. Enjoy it.

Did you stop thinking about your loved one for a few minutes while you were concentrating on your surroundings? Did you get a sense that you're a part of something larger, something wondrous? That your loved one was too? That we're all interconnected in a giant circle?

Many naturalists, environmentalists, ecologists, and animal rights activists are atheists, agnostics, or secular humanists; Sir David Attenborough, Richard Dawkins, Francis Crick, and Ernst Mayr are just a few. Why do you suppose that is?

1 3

$\mathcal{P}$ E T S

$\mathcal{B}$e careful before you rush out and get a dog, a cat, or a bird. Moreover, never get an animal for a grieving friend or family member without talking to that person first.

Pets are not disposable. If you decide after the fact that a pet is too much for you to care for or that you didn't really want it, you will face a painful decision. If you have grieving children, giving away a pet could be traumatic.

Allow me to share my after-Eric's-death pet story with you. Please keep in mind that I was a zookeeper, then a zoo education specialist. I love a variety of animals, and I don't mind making up diets for them and cleaning up after them. I'm also an extremely tactile person—touching and petting animals gives me immense joy. Don't panic. This is not a sad giving-away story.

Onward with the tale . . .

My sister Patty, a medical doctor and dog owner, convinced me after the accident that my two daughters needed a dog. At the time of Eric's death, we had a bunny and a small parrot. When visiting Patty years before the accident, Tia and Robin had fallen in love with her Maltese, Fluffy. Patty wanted to get them a dog just like Fluffy; she had located a breeder, offered to crate-train the puppy, and then bring her as a Christmas present—only five weeks after Eric's death. She thought it would be good for the girls, and without thinking about it, I agreed.

It was a good thing I was an animal person. The Maltese puppy turned out to be a naughty biter and was difficult to potty train. She was cute, though: she looked like a cotton ball someone had put in a clothes dryer and then attached big black eyes to. However, this bundle of white fluff also came with razor-sharp teeth. By the end of Christmas Day, Tia and Robin cowered atop the sofa, begging me to give her back.

Fast-forward to a year later. The puppy, named Nicky by my father-in-law, became the most important being in Tia's life. Nicky lost those puppy teeth, was potty trained, and had turned into the sweetest dog I'd ever known. Many years later I used her as a demonstration dog in classes with mentally challenged children because she was so gentle. She babysat tiny chicks, allowed a guinea pig to curl between her paws, and never destroyed a single item in my home.

As of the writing of this book, Nicky has been to a half dozen vets and has had an ultrasound, a liver biopsy, and countless blood tests. She's presently on several medications, and we think she's going to live, but it has cost thousands of dollars. The medication is expensive, and Nicky may have to be on it for life. Tia and Robin, now young adults, demanded, "Save Nicky, no matter how much it costs." Perhaps their desperate reaction was tied to my husband's death; Nicky was born just days prior to Eric's accident, and she'd come to symbolize much.

I did everything possible for Nicky, including committing large sums of money. Think carefully about this. Do you have the money and the means to care for a dog? I had another dog, a cairn terrier named Toto, who had epilepsy for almost seven years. He required daily medication and still had occasional seizures. When he had a seizure, I become one with my mop. He ruined countless rugs due to uncontrollable loss of bodily functions. Are you willing to take care of a sick animal? Sadly, Toto died in March 2013; I still miss my beautiful pup.[1]

I know people who've spent close to $10,000 on a dog who died anyway. Admittedly, that's a worst-case scenario, but don't think it can't happen to you. Toto's bills from the emergency room clinic on the night he died were well over a thousand dollars. If the vet tells you he or she can save your dog or other pet, but it will cost a considerable sum, what will you do? If there are children involved, it can be a traumatic experience.

Birds and other exotics can be particularly pricey to care for. Don't forget special diets—parrots should not eat seeds except as an occasional treat. Reptiles can be problematic and in my opinion do not make good pets for children. I own a couple of reptiles, and unless you're willing to ensure they have proper light and heat (and in the case of some reptiles like bearded dragons, live food), a reptile is not the pet for you. Chinchillas and hedgehogs are delicate animals and are prone to illness, even when properly cared for. Sugar gliders and monkeys? Don't do it.

If you decide on a cat, please vow to keep it indoors. Free-roaming cats have a devastating impact on wildlife—particularly birds.[2] Additionally, indoor cats enjoy longer life spans. Tia's cat, Jelly, never goes outdoors and is happy and healthy.

---

[1] For more about Toto, see Carol Fiore, "Lessons from a Terrier," *Grief Digest* 10, no. 4 (2013): 6-8.

[2] For more information, see the American Bird Conservancy's Cats Indoors program, http://www.abcbirds.org/abcprograms/policy/cats/index.html.

Rabbits, with their delicate backs, are a poor choice for small children. Squeezing them can literally kill them. Hamsters often bite, and birds are completely inappropriate for kids (and for many adults—especially smokers). At Easter, resist the urge to buy those cute baby chicks and ducks. I have a pet duck—a rescue that came with a deformed wing. Ducks are messy animals and have an average lifespan of around ten years. Do you have a farm, and are you willing to commit to many years of care?

Consider a guinea pig, which can often be a good choice for children. They're sturdy animals, usually gentle if treated kindly, and their cage doesn't need a lid. Their urine can be a bit smelly, so you'll have to clean the cage regularly. Robin had a guinea pig named Pippin who was a wonderful pet. However, never *ever* buy a pet for a child unless you're willing to care for it.

Now that I've told you the reasons not to acquire a pet, allow me to talk about a few of the good things. Dogs will force you to get out of the house and take a walk. They'll greet you with love and wet kisses. They'll miss you when you're gone. They're natural clowns. My daughter Robin thinks a roomful of squeezable puppies could ease many problems—even grief.

In all cases, consider rescuing an animal. It can be extremely rewarding to adopt a homeless pet. Did I mention that Tia's cat, Jelly, is a shelter rescue? There are many farm animals, like goats, sheep, chickens, pigs, and horses, in need of homes too; but keep in mind that these will require a lot of space—ideally, a farm—and a good deal of upkeep.

Studies have shown that pets reduce stress and even extend their owner's lives.[3] My cockatoo knows when I'm sad, and her

---

[3] See, for example, "Studies Show Pets Improve Your Health," http://suite101.com/a/studies-show-pets-improve-your-health-a100443; and Erin Courtenay, "Pet Therapy Provides Far-Reaching Health Benefits for Older Adults," http://www.everydayhealth.com/longevity/emotional-wellness/pet-therapy.aspx.

vocalizations become softer as she burrows into my shoulder. My duck makes me laugh—she even knows her name and goes on walks with the dog and me. My pets make me feel special and useful; I would be lost without them.

If you have no plans to acquire a pet, skip this next task. If you already have a pet, take time to enjoy it. Pets are a wonderful source of comfort—but then, you already know that.

TASK #15

You're determined to adopt a pet. Get on the Internet and read everything you can about the animal. Visit your local library or bookstore. Read; then read some more. Can you care for the animal for its entire life? Can you afford this pet? Does it need a special diet? If it's an exotic, is there a vet in town who cares for this species? Call the vet. How much does a routine checkup cost?

There are additional points to investigate: What is the overall cost of having this animal? What's its average life span? Does it need a special cage, heat, or lighting? What are the cleaning requirements that go with owning it? If you're a renter, is this pet allowed? Are there local ordinances or state restrictions against this animal? Do you have a pet sitter or someone who can watch the animal when you're away?

If you're getting this pet for a child, ask yourself this important question: If my child tires of the pet (and that is likely to happen), am I willing to care for it myself? If the answer is no, then do not adopt the animal.

PET NOTES

Perhaps your beloved pet has died and that's why you're reading this book. Never feel guilty for grieving about an animal. A friend of mine recently lost her dog and was afraid to express too much sadness in my presence because "you lost your husband and that's worse." Yes, I lost my husband, but why should that have anything to do with my friend's expression of grief over her dog? When one of my many pets dies, you can bet I will cry and miss it terribly. This has nothing to do with the loss of my husband; it doesn't take away from it in any way. I am capable of loving many people and many animals. Don't let anyone say you shouldn't grieve for your dog or cat—or even your pet gerbil. Animals are an important part of our lives, and they can quickly become family.

14

BACK TO LIFE, BACK TO WORK

Back to work? *Not yet!* You aren't ready, but perhaps your financial situation won't allow you to take any more time off. You're going to lose everything unless you get back to work. You may have unbelievable medical bills, not to mention funeral costs.

It's probably going to be painful, or at least awkward and uncomfortable. Coworkers will swarm you with advice or hide from you. Even when they aren't mentioning your loved one, or actively avoiding you, their sad looks will be a reminder.

When my husband was dying, my employer sent someone to the hospital to take back my work key. This was my dream job, so

I was devastated. Nonetheless, I don't regret my decision to stay at the hospital with Eric.

I didn't go back to work for well over a year. When I did, I'd moved to a different state, taking a job in another field. Everyone's situation is different. Finances may force you back to work almost immediately. You'll get through it, though it may not be easy. Or maybe you actually want to go back to work because working helps with your grief.

I remember being confused about why everyone was going about the day normally. The sun still came up in the morning, the stores were still open, and people were still going to work. Didn't they understand that this tragedy had happened and the world would never be the same again? Couldn't they see that Eric was never coming back?

No. They didn't.

People tend to express their sorrow and then go back to their lives. It isn't that they don't care, but they didn't love the person as you have. They can't know, even if they say they do. Try to remember, it's difficult for your coworkers too; they don't know how to respond or what to say. Forgive them if they don't act properly. There's bound to be a comment or two about "God's plan."

Getting back to your "old" life as you knew it might be impossible. It's gone. You have to reinvent yourself now. If you have the option to take off work for a while, I would suggest doing so. It may not be the right time to switch jobs unless you're financially secure. Think carefully before you do anything drastic. Perhaps this next task will help.

TASK #16

Write a brief letter to your coworkers. What would you like to say to them? Do you want them to talk about your loved one? Would you rather focus on your job and not talk about your loss? What could they do to bring you some comfort? What would make this less awkward for you and for them?

Do you have a good relationship with your supervisor? Perhaps you could discuss some of the things you just wrote. I believe in the goodness of most people, and it could be that your supervisor wants to help but is unsure what to do.

The letter is actually for you; that's why there's a blank page in this book for you to write on. It may or may not be a good idea to give it to your coworkers; that's for you to decide.

A Letter to My Coworkers

1 5

MAKING A BIG DECISION: SHOULD I MOVE?

*I*f you have a choice, you probably shouldn't move for at least a year. One of my dearest friends did not have a choice, however; after her husband died, she discovered they were in serious debt. There was no life insurance. She lost her big, gorgeous house and her cars. She had two young daughters to support and no money. She decided to stay in the same town because she had family, but she had to move to a smaller place. She did it, though, and I'm extremely proud to call her my friend. She later remarried, and her daughters are doing well.

Eric insisted I wait for a year before moving if he died. He had a good reason for that request. I can be quite naive, and he was afraid someone would take advantage of me, especially if I was profoundly sad. I believe he thought a year would be enough time for me to deal with the grief and be in a position to make good decisions. I moved exactly one year and one day after his death, but it didn't prevent me from being the victim of fraud. We're all different, and my grief was severe. A year was not long enough.

You've had enough change in your life. Moving, perhaps changing jobs, leaving friends and familiar surroundings, and selling and buying a new home are all huge sources of stress. Can you handle it? If you don't have to do it, wait. I thought I could handle the move; I felt I had valid reasons for leaving. Thirteen years later, I still look back and realize I would have had to move at some point. But for me, buying a new home and moving to a different state after only a year was too soon. I was on antidepressants and not thinking clearly. I allowed real estate agents to push through the sale of a new home. My agent failed to look out for my best interests in her hurry to receive her commission. The sellers committed fraud, but I didn't learn of it until years later, when the county planning department threatened me with legal action over violations in existence before I bought the property. It was a nightmare. I discovered the sellers had lied about a multitude of things, and I spent large sums of money fixing things that were broken or not up to code. Although I filed a formal complaint with the state against the sellers' real estate agent—who I'm convinced knew about the defects and code violations—the case was dismissed. The male seller died a few years ago, and suing his grieving widow was not something I could bring myself to do. I was (and still am) angry, but when she showed up on my doorstep crying about him, I invited her in for tea.

Learn from my mistake; don't move until you're in control. Don't buy a house unless you're strong enough to protect your rights; don't rely on a family member to do it for you. Have you investigated the neighborhood? The schools? The crime rate? If I ever buy another house, I will not trust the inspector recommended by the real estate agent. I'll find my own inspector and carefully check out the person's credentials. I'll also hire a licensed electrician and a plumber, again carefully checking out their qualifications. I'll visit the local planning department to check code violations. I'll even run a background check on the sellers or, at a minimum, do a search on the Internet. Excessive? Perhaps. But even if you're planning to rent, you must do your homework. A year can be a long time to lock yourself into a lease in an undesirable location or a home that has problems.

Why are you moving? Is it to be near family? To get out of a town full of painful memories? Because of a new job? Or are you moving because you heard the weather was milder in the new location? Think about the reasons and go to the next task.

TASK #17

Get a pen and fill in the next two pages.

The top of the first page is labeled "Reasons to Leave." The second page is labeled "Reasons to Stay."

Start by listing your reasons for leaving; number your list, and include even minor things.

Now, work on the reasons to stay. Think of all the things you'll be leaving behind if you move: a hairdresser you adore, comfortable surroundings, a secure dwelling, good friends, good schools, and so on.

Compare the two pages. Don't just look at which list is longer. Think about the most important thing you've written down. If you love your job, should you really leave? If you need your friends, should you leave them? Perhaps you've never liked the town, and you feel a fresh start away from the tragedy would help you heal.

Put the pages away and think about them. Come back to them in a week and reread them, perhaps adding a few more things. If you're in doubt about what to do, then I suggest you stay where you are for now. You can always leave later, but if you leave too soon and regret it, it may be difficult (and expensive) to return.

REASONS TO LEAVE

REASONS TO STAY

I've already told you I moved, but you might be wondering if it was a difficult decision. No, it was not. Although I should have waited two or three years, I knew I had to go. My reasons-to-leave list was much, much longer than my reasons-to-stay list. I had no family where Eric and I lived; we had moved there because he'd gotten a test pilot job. The area was much too conservative for me, and I didn't like the weather and the lack of wildlife. The accident was highly publicized, and I found I couldn't go anywhere without people recognizing me. My employer had taken my key when I wouldn't leave the hospital to go back to work, and even though I loved my job, I knew I could not forgive his actions and reapply for my old position. I lived just a few miles from the accident site, and I had to pass by it frequently to get to certain parts of town.

For me, moving was a simple decision and one I don't regret. The timing was the problem. If only I'd waited a year or two longer. If only I hadn't bought *this* house.

16

GETTING RID OF STUFF

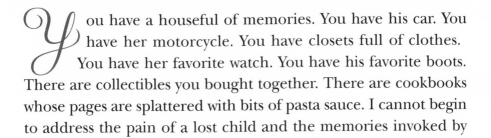

You have a houseful of memories. You have his car. You have her motorcycle. You have closets full of clothes. You have her favorite watch. You have his favorite boots. There are collectibles you bought together. There are cookbooks whose pages are splattered with bits of pasta sauce. I cannot begin to address the pain of a lost child and the memories invoked by stuffed toys and treasured games. Perhaps a parent or sibling has died and you must join with others in disposing of items.

What do you do with it all? If you've lost a spouse or partner and you've been together for a while, the sheer number of things can be overwhelming. Should you give them all away? Sell them? Send them to friends? There's no rush. Wait. Give it some time.

His sister wants the antique clock. Her cousin wants the tan wool jacket. They've asked for things a few times. Here's all you need to say: "Please give me time, and I'll let you know." Recall what we covered in chapter 2: don't put a time constraint on your grief.

In the early days after Eric died, I gave away many of his treasured things. I wanted everyone to have something to remember him by. When people requested items, I turned them over without a thought. He had many possessions, I reasoned, and I could part with some of them. I regret giving away only one item, but I cannot ask for it back. So, *think*. Don't rush into anything.

There are clothes that will never fit and books you'll never read. What should you do with them? Unless you're moving, there's no hurry. Perhaps it brings you comfort to see them. If not, box them up and store them. You can deal with them later.

I preferred to give away my husband's clothes rather than sell them, but there is nothing wrong with selling things. Before you get rid of anything, ask family and friends what they might want. Again, once you donate or sell your loved one's belongings, it will be too late. Think about giving donation items to the loved one's favorite charity; what would that person want you to do with them?

I made a large box for each of my girls with items special to my husband. So far, the boxes are still in my house, but someday they'll retrieve them. Perhaps it won't be until I'm gone; perhaps it will be next year. The boxes are remembrance capsules of their father as a young, vibrant man. They were children when he died, and I feel that the boxes are a way of knowing him better. They contain things like cycling jerseys, airplane logbooks, letters he wrote, military medals, flying scarves, and favorite books. You may want to consider making a remembrance capsule for various family members or friends, when you're able. Again, give yourself time.

Don't do the next task until you're ready to go through your loved one's things. It may take a long time, or you may be ready days or weeks after the death. It took me thirteen years—not until very recently—before I could give away the last of my husband's clothes.

TASK #18

Make a list of special friends or family members who you think may want items. Consider a remembrance capsule for each of them. If a person has requested a particular item, write that down. If you can't part with the item, then don't; think of something else. Set the list aside. Reread it in a few days and cross through any items you can't part with.

When you're ready, pack the boxes. You may wish to include a personal note or decorate the boxes with pictures, drawings, or short sayings. My guess is that the recipient will be overwhelmed by your kindness. Maybe you'd like to invite people over individually to give them the boxes. Or maybe it will be easier for you to distribute them in a group setting. Perhaps merely dropping them off or mailing them suits you better.

$\mathcal{I}$TEMS TO $\mathcal{G}$IVE $\mathcal{A}$WAY

Name of friend/family	Requested item	Other items

Here are some ideas for a remembrance capsule.

- Books; consider buying a copy of your loved one's favorite book for each box.
- Music, favorite movies; you may wish to purchase copies, as I did.
- Letters or something meaningful handwritten by the deceased.
- Small statues or collectibles. As a pilot, Eric had scores of small aviation mementos.
- Clothes like scarves and hats; perhaps a treasured pair of gloves.
- Inexpensive jewelry like tie tacks, pins, earrings, or cuff links.
- Photos; scan copies instead of parting with the originals, and consider special framing.
- Items you have in excess. Eric had several boxes of military patches, so it was easy to part with some of them.

Gather the items together. Can you fit them in a basket, box, or plastic container?

If you're artistic, decorate the container; perhaps attach a picture. Search the Internet for short poems or expressions that aren't religious. Or write something yourself.

ITEMS FAMILY AND FRIENDS DON'T WANT

Now you must decide: sell or donate? If you have the time to advertise and sell, then do so. Take out an ad in the local paper or advertise online. You may find interested buyers at work.

If you decide to donate and your loved one didn't have a favorite charity, check for nonprofit organizations in your town or on the Internet. There are numerous organizations willing to pick up donations from your home. Give them a call.

Should you hold a garage sale? Will friends help with it? Can you deal with strangers picking through your loved one's possessions? I could not have done this, but you're not me. Think about it first and decide if you can handle it emotionally.

Finally, have no regrets. Let it go. It's just *stuff*. The one item I initially regretting parting with was only a thing and not nearly as important as the memories of Eric that I will always have.

17

BEWARE OF RIP-OFF ARTISTS

friend who suffered a tragedy says she doesn't like to tell people about it because they won't care and they might try to take advantage of her. Although I had always been an optimist before Eric died, I admit I find myself struggling at times to believe in the goodness of people. It isn't because I think they don't care; I actually believe that most people think mine is a sad story. What kills the optimist inside me are the people who know yet purposely try to profit from my grief, as I believe the sellers of my new home did.

I've already told you that my new house had a multitude of defects, many of them major. Repair workers had to be hired, and the majority of them ripped me off. Between the workers who charged twice the agreed-upon rate and the ones who did a shabby job, I became frustrated, angry, and bitter. Every one of these people knew I was a widow, and I believe that influenced their prices and the quality of their work. Try doing what I failed to do—hide your situation. Can a competent-sounding friend be present during home repairs?

After Eric died, I became angry that so many people—including two family members—wanted money from me. Even switching the cars and house into my name required checks to the appropriate agencies. Eric had written a will that left everything to me. What if the car or bank accounts were in his name, not mine, and there had been no will? Who would get them? The state? The federal government? I'm not an attorney, but I imagine a complicated mess would result from the absence of a will. Although this falls out of the category of grieving, a word of advice: have a will in place; a simple one is inexpensive.

If, like me, you're not good at fixing things, then this next task is directed at you. If you're like Eric and can repair almost anything, skip this next task.

TASK #19

You need to hire someone to do a job. Do the following, if possible.

- Get a description of the work and the price in writing.
- Incidentally, what does it mean if a company or person advertises as a "Christian" company?
- Check out the company online. Read reviews and the Better Business Bureau's files. Read ratings on sites like Angie's List.[1] Is the company insured? Does it contract out the work? Does it run background checks on subcontracted workers?
- Get a second bid. If in doubt, get a third.
- Ask friends for a recommendation, but don't hire someone solely on that basis.
- Is the company licensed or accredited? Plumbers, electricians, and other professionals have trade associations that can mark them as competent. Also, check with your individual state to see if the contractor is licensed.
- Supervise the work. Check up on the workers. Get a friend to help.
- When the work is complete, insist on getting a professional inspection before you pay the final bill.
- Did you consult with your local planning department to see if a permit was required? Don't try to bypass this; it will lead to trouble.

---

[1] Angie's List, http://www.angieslist.com.

REPAIR WORK NOTES

I know I'm going to receive hate mail over this next statement, but I need to say it: beware of small companies listed as LLCs (limited liability companies). The law protects their personal assets, and if you have a problem, sometimes the company will dissolve and re-form under a different name. You won't be able to touch it or anyone involved. This happened to me concerning a bad floor installation. I was never able to recover any money, and I still have a faulty floor. I now go with the big companies because I have more recourse if they do a poor job. I know we need to support small businesses, but sometimes there isn't much protection for consumers.

There are thousands of ways people can take advantage of you. Be wary of anyone who wants personal information, and never, *never* give it over the phone. Monitor your bank accounts and credit cards closely. If you pay bills over the Internet, use strong passwords and change them regularly. Don't allow strangers access to your computer, and be careful about entering passwords on shared devices (computers in libraries, schools, and hotels).

There are phony charities,[2] phony investments,[3] and phony insurance companies. Contact your state's attorney general if you believe you've been a fraud victim. Report crimes. Because you're not a believer, you'd probably never consider seeing a psychic who claims to be able to contact your dead loved one, but one may try to get in touch with you. Anyone can read an obituary, and sadly, there are rotten people out there who will take advantage of you in your grief. Don't let them.

---

[2] For information on both good and bad charities, go to Charity Navigator (http://www.charitynavigator.org), Guidestar (http://www.guidestar.org), or the Better Business Bureau's charity reviews (http://www.bbb.org/charity-reviews/national).

[3] See the Financial Fraud Enforcement Task Force's website at http://www.stopfraud.gov.

18

Volunteering and Charity Work

*H*elping others helps you. Don't frown; it really is true. When you're doing something meaningful to better another's life, it's uplifting and satisfying. Like anyone else, atheists do much charity work; whether atheists are more generous than religious people is often debated.[1] The problem for everyone when considering charity work is finding the time and having the resources to allow it.

Are you ready? I'm going to repeat myself because it's important: helping others is a way of helping yourself, especially when you're grieving. You'll probably discover others who are suffering; I did.

---

[1] See, for example, http://www.patheos.com/blogs/friendlyatheist/2013/11/28/are-religious-people-really-more-generous-than-atheists-a-new-study-puts-that-myth-to-rest.

You may not have time for volunteer work. Perhaps you lost your house. You're working two jobs. You're raising children alone. This chapter may not be for you—*yet.* Come back to it if or when you can.

If you're still with me, I'll assume you're at least curious about how this might help you. Perhaps you're a regular volunteer already. Only you can say whether you feel up to returning to the job. I'm sure the organization will understand if you take time off. You may decide you can't face returning to your position. Perhaps it's time for something new. Here are just a few ideas.

Working with people.

- Contact your local or regional United Way office and ask about volunteer opportunities.[2]
- Is there a homeless shelter in your town?
- Schools often take on volunteers to assist teachers. Perhaps you could help tutor, mentor, or aid in after-school sports and theater activities.
- Local libraries usually have story-hour sessions for children and frequently need readers.
- Is there a senior center in your town?
- I worked with Meals on Wheels—a wonderful organization that delivers meals to homebound seniors.[3]
- Most cities have soup kitchens, food pantries, and thrift shops for folks needing assistance. Many of these rely on volunteers.
- Do you have a background in art or theater? There may be opportunities for you to help with local productions or assist in a museum.

---

[2] United Way, http://www.unitedway.org.
[3] Meals on Wheels Association of America, http://www.mowaa.org.

- HospiceNet is an outstanding organization;[4] however, it may not be the best choice for you right now, as it may require you to deal with death and dying. As a wildlife rehabilitator, I had a difficult time watching animals die, so I know I couldn't have worked with terminally ill people. Even now, years later, I'm not sure I could do it. But you're not me, and this might be a good fit for you. Hospitals often take volunteers as well.
- Use the Internet to search for volunteer opportunities in your city.

Working with animals and nature.

- Call your city's parks and recreation department to find out about volunteer possibilities such as cleaning up litter, raking leaves, overseeing open spaces, or assisting with disaster relief.
- If you live close to wildlife areas or parks, the city or county may hire summer guides. Often there are opportunities to work with kids teaching them about nature.
- Work with a nonprofit animal rights or environmental group. Have you considered lobbying? Contact your local chapter of the Sierra Club.[5]
- Is there an animal shelter or wildlife rehabilitation facility near you? They usually take volunteers.
- Do you live near a zoo? This type of volunteer work usually requires a substantial commitment; ask first, and make sure you are up to the challenge.
- Many cities have nature preserves or other wildlife centers or museums. See if they take volunteers.

---

[4] HospiceNet, "Volunteers," http://hospicenet.org/html/volunteer.html.
[5] Sierra Club, http://www.sierraclub.org.

TASK #20

Before you skip this task, ask yourself the following question, and be honest: Am I really too busy to volunteer a few hours a week to help the environment or other people?

If you're supporting kids and working a full-time job, then you get a pass. Move on to the next section. But someday, when you're able, think seriously about helping your community.

Look at the preceding lists. Are you more interested in helping people or animals? Pick at least one thing on the list, or search the Internet to find something I didn't include.[6] Make a phone call and see if there's a volunteer opportunity that interests you. If you decide to help, give yourself at least three sessions before you decide to stay or leave.

Go you! You're trying to help others, which is no small task when you're suffering.

---

[6] The website http://foundationbeyondbelief.org calls themselves "compassionate humanists supporting charities worldwide."

NOTES ON VOLUNTEER WORK

I've done volunteer work my whole life, starting as a kid when I was a candy striper at the local hospital. In college, I washed airplanes for the local flight club. When my husband was in the military, I organized events and parties. When I had kids, I coached soccer, held offices in the parent-teacher organization, and was a Brownie troop leader for the Girl Scouts. I was a zoo volunteer for years before being hired as a keeper.

After Eric died, I did nothing for well over a year. My first volunteer job was making food trays for our local Meals on Wheels, but I missed animals and eventually started volunteering in wildlife rehabilitation. When the facility offered me a job as a humane educator, I took it. Working with wildlife was different from working at a zoo. Injured and orphaned wild animals often die, despite our best efforts. Covered in dirt and sweat, I often cried in the back room. The emotional toll of watching the death of so many animals I had worked hard to save began to break me, just when I was beginning to heal.

Today I teach free environmental education classes in the community. I've done some lobbying, signed petitions to protect habitats and animals, helped with fieldwork to save prairie dogs, and given speeches and written articles. I have never received money for any of these endeavors; I do it because my volunteer work helps the community, other people, my animal friends, and myself. Each of us has a choice about the type of life we want to live.

Choose to lead a giving, ethical life.

19

Memorials, and a Short Note about Nonreligious Funerals

Here are some ideas for honoring a loved one.

- Set up a scholarship fund.
- Conduct a sporting event like a road race or cycling event.
- Have a plaque erected at a favorite place (a zoo, a school, a local park).
- Set up a fund to help find a cure for a disease or illness.
- Lobby to enact safer laws to prevent tragic accidents.
- Donate books to a library; place bookplates inside the covers in memory of your loved one.

- Set up a display at a local art or other museum.
- Set up a website or Facebook page in memory of your loved one.

There are thousands of ways to honor someone's memory. Perhaps the best way is to keep your loved one alive in you. My wonderful grandfather, William Mayer, used to tell me he would never be dead as long as I remembered him. That doesn't mean you have to do everything someone would have wanted; you do not have to adopt a loved one's likes and dislikes or go into the same career field. Don't become a doctor solely because late uncle Ted would have wanted it. You need to be you.

I set up a scholarship at the Kansas Cosmosphere and Space Center in Hutchinson, Kansas, in Eric's memory.[1] Truthfully, it took a considerable amount of money and you may not be able to manage that. I tried to set one up at our alma mater, but I didn't have the funds for a full scholarship at the time; perhaps one day I will. Even so, people occasionally contribute money for books or other things in Eric's name.

I also started a program for burn patients at the hospital where Eric died; unfortunately, the funds ran out. I paid to have a plaque erected at the home of the Experimental Aircraft Association in Oshkosh, Wisconsin, and I donated Eric's flying equipment for two displays—one at our alma mater, Parks College of Engineering, Aviation and Technology of St. Louis University,[2] and the other at the Cosmosphere. I also created a webpage to honor Eric,[3] and began working on the book *Flight through Fire*, which has subsequently been published.

---

[1] Kansas Cosmosphere and Space Center, http://www.cosmo.org.

[2] Parks College of Engineering, Aviation and Technology of St. Louis University, http://parks.slu.edu/.

[3] "A Celebration of a Hero: Eric E. Fiore," http://www.carolfiore.com/starteric.html.

The most important way I keep Eric's memory alive is by telling people about him and talking about him with our daughters. Not a day passes when one of us doesn't say, "Daddy would have loved that . . ." or, "Do you remember when Daddy . . . ?"

My grandpa was right. If people remember you, then you will never really be gone.

Task #21

How do you want people to remember you? Write down some ideas. Read them.

When you're better, take steps to make them happen.

How I Want to Be Remembered

Originally I didn't intend to discuss funerals and services because I assumed that you, my reader, would not be looking for grief help until later, after these events had passed. It seemed unnecessary to discuss something that has already happened.

However, because so many people have asked me about this, I've decided to add a note here. I find it interesting that the funeral of a skeptic causes so much confusion. "If you don't have it in a church," people ask, "what will you actually do?" Or they will say, their eyes wide, in a breathless voice, "You mean . . . you don't pray for the dead person?" *Gasp!*

Why are people mystified and upset by this? There are many ways to honor a deceased loved one aside from praying. I'll share my story about Eric's service and funeral, and you can decide if we honored his memory well. Perhaps it will leave you with some ideas for your own service when the time comes. It's a good idea to let those closest to you know what you want.

We held Eric's service in a hangar at Mid-Continent Airport in Wichita, Kansas. His "baby," the Bombardier CRJ-700 aircraft, was in the hangar. We lovingly displayed Eric's car racing medals, his cycling equipment, memorabilia from his days flying the F-15 fighter jet, and various other items within the embrace of his "baby." His closed coffin stood at the front of the hangar, surrounded by large posters of him smiling and hamming it up in the cockpit. Family members, including Tia and Robin, spoke. My eulogy included a line about how Eric claimed to have married me because I didn't puke in his plane.

At my request, all the pilots wore flight suits. A microphone traveled through the crowd of more than four hundred friends as they told stories of Eric's exploits. A short video aired while "our" song—"Wild Horses," by the Rolling Stones—played.

As a former F-15 fighter pilot, Eric was extremely proud of his military service, so he'd asked for military honors when he died.

The air force made sure it happened. I requested a flyover, but I was told it couldn't take place. However, as the hangar doors rose for the firing of the military guns, a jet streaked by the open doors. The air force denied having arranged it, as did my husband's company, Bombardier. I never found out who was flying, but my daughters and I wish to thank the pilot.

People came to our house after the service for food and drinks, and we toasted Eric and told more stories about him.

He would have loved it.

Eric, originally from New York, is buried in a military cemetery near Albany. Stunning farmland and grazing cows surround it. Just a few months before the accident, Eric had cycled there and later remarked to his parents about how beautiful the area was. The funeral service for Eric was a celebration of a remarkable, caring man.

An atheist.

20

THE WONDERS OF TRAVEL

*I*f you're able to get away, and you feel comfortable doing so, then a change of environment, away from painful memories, can be healing. Maybe it's just across town to a friend's house. Some of us can't bear to leave so soon—being surrounded by familiar things is comforting and the thought of going away is unsettling. There are others, lucky enough to have the means, who feel the need to travel. I don't use the word travel in the sense that others do. Being a *traveler* is something much more than being a tourist.

Travelers don't simply "go on vacation" or "get away"; they embark on journeys that change their lives. When travelers go to the beach, they aren't passive lumps on the sand; they're keen observers who interact with native peoples and learn about the area and the ecosystem. They become an active part of the experience and thus often gain a different perspective on their own lives. They re-create themselves with every new trip.

The best travelers aren't rich, just creative; in fact, they can often be quite frugal. Staying at five-star hotels and ordering room service aren't experiences for most travelers; trekking to a remote village in Romania and baking bread with natives is. If you want to be a traveler, then you may have to say no to expensive cars and frivolous purchases in order to save for trips.

Because I'm an atheist, I don't believe in an exotic afterlife; the only amazing trips I'm going to take are the ones I create here and now. Careful planning and reading, searching for deals on airfare and hotels, and setting money aside every month has allowed me to become a traveler. But let me start at the beginning.

My father was in the US Air Force, and in addition to living all over the United States, the family lived in England and in Turkey. As a child, I frequently ran off to the outer fence of Incirlik Air Force Base near Adana, Turkey, and stared sadly at the children on the other side who wore ragged clothes and lived in huts without bathrooms or running water. I tried to slip food through the fence to them. Because I almost never left the base, I believed the Turks lived inside a big fence, rather than the other way around.

Once, before we left Turkey, my father took me to downtown Adana. I saw begging children covered in sores, dead dogs in the street, markets with fly-covered meat. My world changed forever; *I* changed forever. Curiosity and empathy arose in me, and I vowed to see as much of the world and other cultures as I could. I've met other "military brats" who found they were bitten by the travel bug too.

When Eric joined the air force, I had one request: to live abroad. My goal to become a traveler had been put on hold too long. I will always be grateful to our military for allowing Eric to fly the F-15 and for sending us to the beautiful Netherlands for three incredible years. I finally began to make my dream a reality as I dragged Eric around Europe at every possible opportunity. We had little money, but by searching for deals and being flexible, we had adventures galore. We skied in Austria, ate pastries in Vienna, traipsed around the British Isles, sipped wine in Paris, laughed with the locals in Rome, and immersed ourselves in Dutch culture. I even studied Russian art and architecture in the former USSR. When we returned to the United States, we planned for subsequent trips to our favorite places abroad, to see people we'd met or to finish hikes we'd barely started.

About a year after Eric died, my sister convinced me to return to the Netherlands, to see the house we'd lived in, the courses I'd run on, the base where he'd flown his beloved F-15. It was emotionally difficult but healing. I returned again in 2009 to run, once again, in the Rotterdam Marathon. I wore a shirt with Eric's picture on it; he had helped me train the first time I ran it back in 1986. With every step, for twenty-six miles, I healed.[1] Every trip, every journey in between and since, has helped with my grief. It was difficult being a traveler without Eric, but I found new traveling buddies— my daughters Tia and Robin.

I went to New Zealand to watch little blue penguins,[2] and hiked in Romania. I returned to Russia and made new friends. I marveled at the vastness of the Australian outback and its charming people, and hiked twenty-one miles on the Appian Way outside Rome. I finally stood in the Athens Agora and stared up at the Parthenon.[3] I tried to learn the languages and speak with the people. I watched the wildlife and fed stray dogs. I gazed at the crumbling ruins of long-dead civilizations and thought of the great minds who'd lived

---

[1] Carol Fiore, "Ik Spreek Nederlands," *Grief Digest* 8, no. 2 (2010): 20–21.
[2] Carol Fiore, "Feathered Hope at the Bottom of the World," *Grief Digest* 7, no. 1 (2009): 28–29.
[3] Carol Fiore, "Greece, at Last," *Grief Digest* 10, no. 2 (2012): 28–29.

and died. I felt grateful to be part of this world, with all its wonders and its incredible people.

I have my favorite places and people, of course, but I love everywhere I've traveled. The United States has its own special majesty; its people are as diverse as those of anywhere I've ever been. I'm quite fond of Tucson, and enjoy hiking in the magnificent Sonoran Desert. I've learned that people around the world are all the same—many of us touched by grief and doing our best to cope in our own ways. I've acquired a new perspective on the world as I've healed and grown. I've become a better person, a better writer, a better mother.

I've never forgotten what it was like to be that little girl in Turkey, so long ago, who just wanted to see the world and meet new people. I wanted to learn, and I have. It is with intense thankfulness that I approach this incredible life of mine. I was fortunate to have been able to embark on many glorious journeys with Eric, and now with my two daughters. Traveling is my great passion, one to which I devote much of my resources.

With a sense of adventure, flexibility, and a bit of humor, you can become a traveler too. You don't have to be rich, and you don't have to go abroad. New experiences and interesting people could be in the next town or park.

21

CLOSURE?

Who first applied the word *closure* to grief? I suspect that person had never suffered from deep, profound grief; anyone who had would have known there's no such thing as closure. We all have different personalities and emotional states, and our circumstances are distinct. That means our grief experience will vary widely—some of us are going to hurt much more than others.

I'm sorry to be the one to say this, my friend, but you may hurt forever. The pain will subside with time, and you'll find you can go for longer periods without thinking about the loved one you lost. But the pain may always be there, lurking in the background, a dull ache.

Grief is an enormous brown bear at the zoo—calm most of the time, but able to erupt without warning. Like the bear, grief may seem to be asleep, harmless. Nevertheless, the right conditions can cause it to attack. A song (*that* song), a movie, or a particular smell are some of the things that can cause grief to come rampaging back, just when you thought it was gone. Grief will burrow into your inner being, out of sight, and climb out when you least expect it. If you know it's hiding, you can be ready for it. Or can you?

TASK #22

Repeat this to yourself: I will have good days; I will have not-so-good days. Overall things will improve, but I will never forget the person I lost. Sometimes the pain will overwhelm me, but I will be okay.

When we love, we expose ourselves, sometimes throwing our whole being straight into the abyss, hoping it's filled with happiness rather than pain. Love ties us to another, and when we lose that person it can be like being run over by a bullet train as we stare dreamily up at fluffy clouds: we never saw it coming.

Time to put the what-ifs behind. We can't change the past; we can only move forward, vowing to learn from our experiences and doing everything we can to live with intention. "Live like it's your last day" isn't a trite expression anymore. We know it; we feel it; we're living it.

Give yourself a big hug. You're doing well.

I've found it helps to have a yearly tradition, something you do on the anniversary of your loved one's death. It can be as simple as planting a tree or flowers. Perhaps on this day you donate time at the local food bank or blood at the local hospital. Maybe you play your loved one's favorite music or watch a special movie. If you have children, ask them if there's something they would like to do.

Of course, you can visit the cemetery, lay flowers on the grave, and say a few words. Maybe you stay and talk for hours. So what if the person can't hear you? If it helps you, then do it.

You might be wondering if I have a yearly tradition. Yes, I do. I always speak to my daughters (usually by phone now that they don't live at home), and we tell stories about their daddy. I usually don't go out that day. In the evening, I read some of Eric's old notes and letters, and I watch a movie. It's the same movie, every year. And I remember that of all the women on the planet, Eric loved *me*. It has taken me over a decade, but I can honestly say that I was lucky. I never thought I'd believe those words. It took a very, *very* long time, but I got better.

You will too.

Life can be difficult and cruel, but it can also be wondrous. Hold tight to that last part. That Eric lived, that he loved me, that we had a beautiful, passionate relationship . . . that was wondrous.

We're all going to die. If we didn't—if we were immortal—then we'd never truly live.

22

$\mathcal{D}$ ATING

his chapter probably isn't for you unless you've lost a spouse or partner, so feel free to skip it. If you've lost a partner, it's your decision whether to date or not. Maybe you want to be independent, at least for a while. Maybe you're the type of person who can't handle being alone and you need a companion. Maybe you're too stressed and busy right now to think about dating.

You can ask for advice, but your family and friends don't get to tell you what to do. Your beloved partner is gone, and he or she is not watching you. You loved the person, but this is your life and you know what's right for you.

If you've recently lost a partner and you have children, do not expose them to dates. I'm not saying you can't date; I'm saying be careful about exposing the children to it for a while. How long is "a while"? It will depend on the ages of the children, your relationship with the child's deceased parent/caregiver, the emotional stability of the children, and possibly other factors. Use good judgment; get professional help if you're unsure or need help making a decision.

Have I waited long enough to date? you may be asking yourself. If you have to ask, you probably have. Consider the feelings of parents, in-laws, and—as mentioned—children. Others can't make decisions for you, but you should pause to consider how your dating might affect them. Proceed with caution.

Relationships are hard enough as it is. When you're still in love with your deceased partner and deeply grieving, entering into a new relationship is probably a bad idea. Give it some time.

There's one other thing I must mention. Be wary of prospective partners who are out to grab the insurance money, abuse the kids, or take advantage of you in some other way. Don't hesitate to run a background check. You can do it discreetly, and there are resources available via the Internet. Tell the other person if you feel guilty about doing it; an ethical person won't mind. If something doesn't feel right about the new relationship, it probably isn't; trust your gut instincts. You may have more at stake than just your heart, so guard yourself well.

When the grieving becomes less painful, that doesn't mean it's time to rush into a relationship. Take some time to be alone with your thoughts. Get to know yourself—the new you that is living without your deceased loved one. So many people are afraid to be alone. Don't be. Stay up late and eat cookies in bed. Stand out on your patio and look at the stars. Don't be in a rush. People are often afraid of introspection, but now is indeed the time to engage in it. It could save you much misery in the future.

I'm not the dating expert—not even close. I only included this chapter because so many people ask, "Have you remarried?"

No, but you know what? It's nobody's business. To date or not to date is *your* decision.

23

TIME

Time is your sympathetic friend.
But.
You never want to will your life away. You are, after all, not a religious person. You know this life is all we get, so don't wish the days away. Yes, it will take time for the pain of loss to subside, but in the meantime, there are things you can do.

Look back at this book's chapter headings if you need a reminder. Exercise, get out in nature, and take comfort from your children and your pets. Perhaps do some charity work and set up a memorial to your loved one. Remake yourself. Try a new hobby or sport. Keep a journal of stories about your loved one. Take a pottery class or play a musical instrument. Learn a foreign language. Travel.

We're not religious. You and I don't believe in an afterlife. This is all we get, my friend. Your loved one is gone; my Eric is gone. But you and I will live our lives, and we'll do the best we can. Some days will suck, but there will be good ones too. Last summer I followed the antics of two exquisite fawns that were born on my property. They returned with their mom this year and I rejoiced in my beautiful Bambis. Take joy in those small things.

The world will appear not to care. Some people will tire of your sad, sad song, but you will find others who support you. Get through each day as well as you can and don't be too hard on yourself. So, you messed up today; so what? Maybe tomorrow will be better and, if not, then maybe next week. Be kind to yourself and know that you are not the only one who has suffered. Did you look into a support group?

I would like to encourage you to read Poem 561 by Emily Dickinson. Although she did not name her poems, others have called it "I measure every grief I meet." The poem is about the grief of others as much as our own grief.[1] You might compare your grief to that of others; I've done it, we all do it. But we shouldn't. We are all unique, with different emotional states, different personalities, and different circumstances. Emily Dickinson spoke to this much more eloquently than I ever can. Poem 561 can easily be found on the Internet if you'd like to read it.

My friend, you are not alone. I wish you tailwinds.

---

[1] Warning: Poem 561 contains a reference to Christ's suffering.

10136076R00075

Printed in Great Britain
by Amazon.co.uk, Ltd.,
Marston Gate.